Prosthetic Gods

by Jonathan Penton

Unlikely Books

www.UnlikelyStories.org
New Orleans, Louisiana

Prosthetic Gods

Cover art by Sri Nash Parker

ISBN 13: 978-0-9708750-5-1

Six Dollars

Prosthetic Gods was originally published in 2008 by Rane Arroyo at
Winged City Chapbooks, an imprint of New Sins Press, with an
ISBN-13 of 978-0-9796956-9-8

This Second Edition published 2013 by:

Unlikely Books

www.UnlikelyStories.org
New Orleans, Louisiana

To these gods he attributed everything that seemed unattainable to his wishes, or that was forbidden to him. One may say, therefore, that these gods were cultural ideals. Today he has come very close to the attainment of this ideal...Man has, as it were, become a kind of prosthetic God. When he puts on all his auxiliary organs he is truly magnificent; but those organs have not grown on to him and they still give him much trouble at times.

—Sigmund Freud, *Civilization and Its Discontents*

your poetry is pure
passionate
physical

every stitch in your paper screams sincere
your ink a mix of sweat, tears, vomit, and blood

trouble is, you've been using my blood

First Mind Buried

It's all very well for Allen to say
        that he knew the best   plural   minds of his generation
but chances are you didn't

chances are you knew punks   frauds   egos   clingons
cheap fucks who rent their stolen suits
chances are
        you only knew one mind
                         worth saving

        chances are it was the first you buried
        chances are good it was not the last

           there is no tape for the way minds break
           there's a million things that can go wrong
           and not one of them is anything
a doctor
        could notice

we seek the solution to madness knowing
sanity has no answers

So you have a little world
And you think your world has meaning
But I take your world
For spite, for sport
So what will you do now?

And you have a little god
And you pray your god has power
But I kill your god
For sport, for spite
So what will you do now?

You're respected at your job
You work in four felt walls
But you can't have a job when I'm around since your hearing
        won't turn down

So you go back to school
To excel as you always do
Campus politics just make you laugh
They'll never reach in you

Still you feel a little small
Fuck your student in the hall
But I taunt you and you hear me still so you fuck her like a queer

But you carve a little niche
You've got room to invite friends
And you cast your thoughts in radii like you perceive a web
Or a crystal when it's dead

        And you lash at the strength of the helpless
        Trapped in the techniques of the weak
And I can't really stop   this little game of vengeance
Until you can lie still on top of me

my lips brush the image of a weak man
i kiss his words
you lie like the innards of a strong man
when your mouth folds into something we can't use
our backs arched on different curves
you kiss like the message of a good man
that neither of us will ever touch
i reach for the body of a memory
that no one thinks of much

So you have a moment
Of true worship
And find what you'd been seeking after forgetting how to look

The moment passes, but you knew they always do
You just weren't certain they'd ever return
You're stronger now, you can wait for the next one—

So you return to your life
conceived, designed, and built in misery
you bring it this ecstasy
and find it has less purpose than before
that waiting seems easy, and seeking seems senseless

Sin of the Calf

Knowing that g-d is found in fucking
That the fuckers don't matter at all
I still try to worship your face
Still look to your actions for my body's use
Your random passions for somebody's truth

Beautiful, broken darling
Goddess soaked in filth
I dump your shit
On the woman I keep
Just to see what I can make grow

Maror

Every night, I think of your betrayal
And the bitterness floods my bag
to form a heavy shelter
That protects me from my enemies
That warms me in dead desire

And every morning, I tear my shelter down
I think only of the warmth of your body
So that I might freeze in the desert sun
I carve your name into the flesh of murderers
To share with them the freshness of my wounds

Yet know this
as she smashes your heart with her fists:

There are no former poets.
There are only poets,
failed poets,
and dead poets,

and only those in the final group can be numbered.

And in that moment
just before your spray
given the options
was it really so much easier to
turn away and face the wall
find comfort in some instant too long gone
and duck the question
of what you and I might represent

decline to comment
on the differences between our then and now
and choose to spend this time away
keep anything I might offer at bay
spend moments staring into space
looking for someplace you won't find
letting me watch as you
seek solitude
the moment
that you
come

Venus walks among us, invisible and stalking.
Men are not her object.
Venus picks women. She chooses them carefully.
They never get away.

Venus picks women. She does not wait 'til they have grown.
She murders their parents.
Parents do not befit a god.
She puts them on the street.
She puts them into alleys.
She puts them in the hands of the state.
She puts them someplace they'll run from,
and she destroys whatever they try to run to.

Venus rapes women. She ravages their faces
                              destroys their hands
                                    mutilates their feet
and when she's ruined   every inch of them save their orifices
she sends a mortal to finish the job

Venus destroys women
usually, Venus kills women

sometimes, Venus takes women
sometimes, Venus fills their tiny bodies
and walks among us   for everyone to see

Shooter's Knob
after Stephen King

when the machismo of your intellect fails you
just smack the bitch around
when you're tired of playing Dirty Harry
try your hand at a murderous spree

      Ain't no one here believe you're a good person, anyway
      Ain't no one thought you that in years
      And if that confuses you
      Don't let it slow you down

once you realize there are no righteous killings
find out if you're the killer   you've always claimed to be

You'll know who you are if you stop yourself
you know who you are if you don't
and I'll tell you now   we're coming for you either way

I'm a Poet Too!

This is the last poem I write about you.
Swear to g-d.
Swear to G-d, this time.

This is the last time I pour whiskey into my coffee cup
    scribbling notes through a poet's reading
because this is the last time I'm in a coffee shop
        when it's past time I should be drinking

    This is the last time I will hesitate before using the C-word
      when not speaking directly to a representative of my local
        police department who is acting in his or her official capacity

    This is the last time that I pretend that I'm ignoring you
    But it is not the last time I pretend that you're ignoring me

Back-alley moralists
Your hearts long severed   from your literary niche
Enlightenment-hobbyists
Who scratch each other's back long past the removal of all skin

    No, I mean it. No more pages of free-verse jabbering about
    what a bunch of losers you are. It's incredibly transparent
    and self-serving. It only degrades me. It's when you read it
    that you degrade

This one reads just like the last one
and I've got a million more

But there's no need to spit out
what's in someone else's mouth
and there's no poetry community
into which poetry can fit

So there's no need for friends or enemies
or comfort in being read
no lovers among your listeners

There's no slice of the market you can eat:
The market will always eat you

She asked me how to improve her poetry

I told her to destroy her lovers, neglect her family, and sit alone and lonely until she can't remember the smell of love, until she can't remember the thrill of beauty, until all she has left is an empty and fossilized truth that can only destroy her in her quest to stifle the Quixotian quests of strangers

She turned away in disgust. Now she has a computer in her family room and writes rhymed verse about her favorite holidays which she sells for $20 a pop to the local community paper

Another crisis I've averted

Another stranger saved

Notyu Journal

tonight it is you i channel
        your mouth in a group of strangers
        your hand on another woman's body

---

                        we compete with one another
            seeking the deepest level of hopelessness

          we always wanted to be great at something

---

i can feel you now
                staring at that blank screen
i want you so badly
    that i get your writer's block

Notyu is a pre-Buddhist Japanese form based on an irrational number of syllables.

on your fingers
i finally catch the scent
of your new lover's ass

i've been sniffing for it
you've kept clean for so long
it's not what i expected

but then, you never were

i leave my own scent in reply
a little camaraderie, a little malice
a little bit of comfort   in knowing
that dogs don't always fight

Don't Let Me Give You a Title

There's a bearded man stretched naked across the foyer floor
and you realize you've reached a place you've only read about
                    in weird fiction   and the biographies of the mad

You move smoothly, easily
among these discharged minds
their walls of blood and puke

Coke on every mirror

Pills in every couch

It's not a party here until somebody's dead
                    Platypus women and weasel men
                    dressed not fashionably, nor like rejects
                    dressed like they can't quite clothe themselves at all
                    match their sense with their socks

                    Separate from society, they have no need to rebel

                    Too close to the source of empathy
                    they've lost the ability to sense
                    any mind but their own
                                        collective
                                            unconsciousness

A lesser extrovert would be terrified
but you feel more you than ever:
this is a fantasy you never understood you had
you hold your liquor
and your water
long after your host is past passing

                    Here, style and grace
                    the only virtues you've known
                    are the only measure of a man

One woman in particular
loves to hear your woundless words
      You grease the thighs between her eyes
      and watch her skin twitch slightly
          under your   superior   selfish   logic
           You let her wrap herself
               into the shapes you want her to need
           and as her moments come to a head
you see a subtle sign—
before unnoticed—
flashing in the corner

             Do not tease the animals.

             Do not tease the animals.

       Although they are not capable of making threats

          This is not a request.

Should they ever write of us
       the lies they tell will be worse for their benevolence
Should they speak of us in hushed tones
       their worship will be false as their fucking

All writers repeat:
         They convince themselves the unique are unhappy
         They see a life of misery and think it a miserable life
         They take a suicide and judge it tragedy
         They immortalize suffering:
                 Our immortal joy won't interest them at all

Let us die together, beloved
Let us do it now, before they determine what to write
Let our immortality be something only lovers share

the rain drenches me at the bus stop
the salsa jar cuts open my hand
Our day care closes in minutes

as the old men march for peace
while the young men march for justice
and the union blames them both
for the price of hot school lunches

you want compassion in my time of labor
you want love from a broken back
i fantasize of sex in the shoah
i wonder what you think We have

Arguing with the War Widow

Her corpses pile like friendships, newspapers,
a stack of obituaries falling over as you try to use the toilet.
Her own rage hidden, she takes up yours for sport

She says, "where there is life, there is hope."
She trembles with hatred when I point out she lies.
She does not believe I have earned certainty.

when i cut myself this way
        it's to know how he bled
        this scar is for her

for each wicked lover
for each evil friend
        i find the way to wound myself until i look like them

You see how much i want to forgive you
You see how many i'm willing to hurt

Thus did Cerridwyn and Jesus fight like Eliot and Pound
While Ché sang to Evita on what matters on the ground
And all their manifestos mean nothing to me now—
Your gods are the biggest joke since the Bible

A failure, celebrated, can never push through
The samsara of gender to seek something true
So if we are all destined to love and to lose
Let me suffer without any comforts
And the lies that you tell to make your lies worth living
Can rot with the flesh of our culture

Take instinct and reason and all our deceit
Take Brando in Paris and take my wife, please
But when you take that money and you fucking leave
Let us both understand what we've come to

We've defiled our flag as fire never could
We've built a stone fortress with tools of bad wood
Our symbols replace that for which they have stood
They shield us from truth and self-torture
But you were never a woman and I was never a man
Our bodies are not what divides us

and still i dream of connection
a calendar of hickeys on my chest
a Messianic Age of every pubis

and now i'm trapped at this party
listening to your idiotic drone
i'm drunk
              of frail body
                              arguing Bergman
smelling your cunt from across the room

Jonathan Penton began adventuring the night of March 14th, 1964, wearing a mask fashioned from the discarded dress of a dead woman with an Italian last name. When the Keene Act was passed in 1977, he left his one-word rebuttal outside a police station, tacked to the body of a multiple rapist. On November 2nd, 1985, he failed to prevent the salvation of the world.

He would like to thank Rofiah Breen, Brad M. Elliot, Vernon Frazer, Lora Gardner, Mary Jo Malo, Brent Powers, Lisa Renee Vincent, and especially Rane Arroyo of New Sins Press for their assistance with this volume.

Some of the poems in *Prosthetic Gods* have appeared, in some cases in a different form, in *The Houston Literary Review*, *Kagablog*, *Kickass Review*, *Penumbra*, and *Unquiet Desperation*.

www.ingramcontent.com/pod-product-compliance
Lightning Source LLC
Chambersburg PA
CBHW030012040426
42337CB00012BA/748